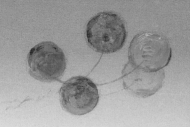

When the Wind Blows

by **Stacy Clark**

illustrated by **Brad Sneed**

Holiday House / New York

This book is dedicated to my friend Pete Seeger, whose stories and songs inspired my love of nature as a child and whose lifelong environmental advocacy inspired this book.—S. C.

To imaginators, innovators, and educators—B. S.

ACKNOWLEDGMENTS
Thanks to my mother, Virgie, for her late-night reviews of this story's myriad iterations. Thanks to my son, Dylan, whose rapid-fire questions about the world and how things work have made parenting *the* adventure of my life. To the scientific and literary friends who, remarkably, have always found the time to answer *my* questions, I appreciate your time and energy tremendously: Mark Z. Jacobson, Michael E. Mann, Paul Hawken, Mark J. Rodgers, Dianna Hutts Aston, Mary Schutte, Andy Ross, Anne-Marie Izac, and the great minds at the National Renewable Energy Laboratory and the St. Mark's School of Texas.

Stacy Clark

The publisher thanks Ramesh Agarwal, PhD, for his expert review of this book.

Library of Congress Cataloging-in-Publication Data
Clark, Stacy.
When the wind blows / by Stacy Clark ;
illustrated by Brad Sneed.
pages cm.
ISBN 978-0-8234-3069-7 (hardcover)
1. Wind—Juvenile literature.
I. Sneed, Brad illustrator. II. Title.
QC931.4.C53 2015
551.51'8—dc23
2013037813

When the wind blows

Porch doors sway

Dune grass bends

Sea waves spray

When the wind blows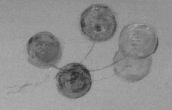

Balloons escape

Beach balls roll

Clouds change shape

When the wind blows

Skippers grin

Sailing offshore

Where windmills spin!

When the wind blows

Blades rotate

Turning gears

Accelerate

When the wind blows
   Copper whirls 'round
      Between two magnets
         High aboveground

When the wind blows

Magnetic forces

Use electrons

As energy sources

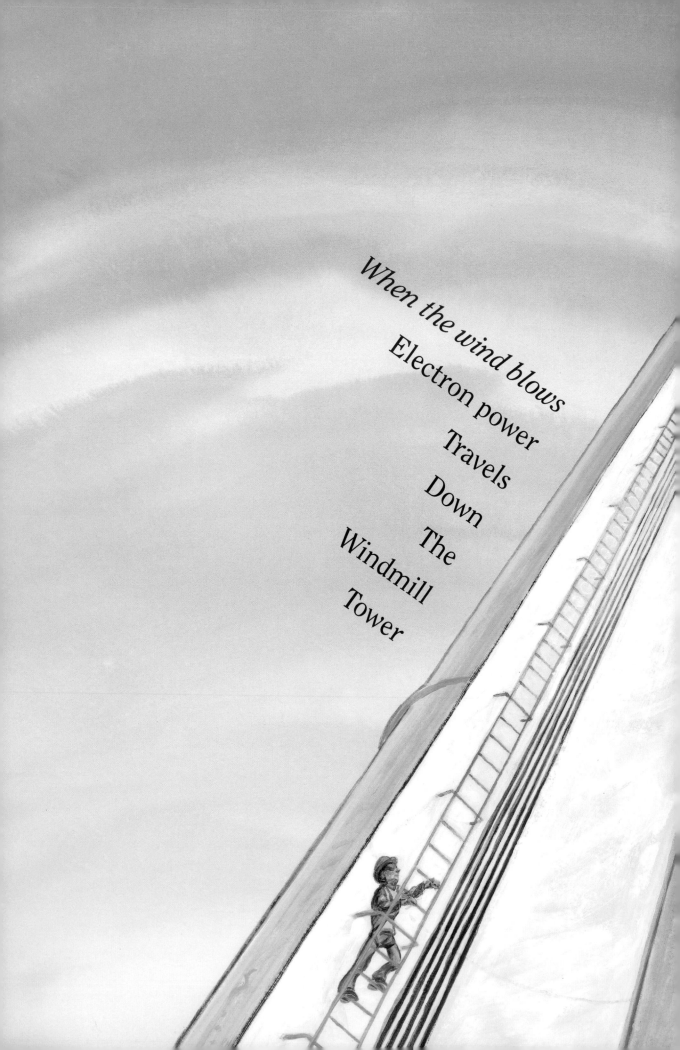

When the wind blows
Electron power
Travels
Down
The
Windmill
Tower

When the wind blows
Circuits ignite
Electricity!
Flows day

And night

When the wind blows
Electrons soar
Through power lines
They arrive onshore

When the wind blows

It powers a station

Charging the grid

That fuels our nation

When the wind blows

It activates lights

Warms cold homes

And cools hot nights

When the wind blows

The lighthouse shines

Signaling ships

Through nighttime

When the wind blows
A whistle blasts!
Electricity
Powers railroad tracks

When the wind blows
Factories hum
Harbors light up
Smart cars run